S OF THE PAST

LOST CITIES

Jason Hook

RAINTREE
STECK-VAUGHN
PUBLISHERS

A Harcourt Company

Austin   New York

Published by Raintree Steck-Vaughn, an imprint of Steck-Vaughn Company.

Library of Congress Cataloging-in-Publication Data

Hook, Jason.
    Lost Cities / Jason Hook
        p.cm. -- (Mysteries of the past)
    Includes bibliographical references and index.
    ISBN 0-7398-4337-0
        1. Extinct cities--Juvenile literature. 2. Cities and towns, Ancient-- Juvenile literature. 3. Civilization, Ancient--Juvenile literature. [1. Extinct cities 2. Cities and towns, Ancient 3. Civilization, Ancient.] I. Title. II. Mysteries of the past.

CC176 .H66 2001
930.1--dc21   2001016097

Raintree Steck-Vaughn Staff: Marian Bracken, Pam Wells
Project Manager: Richard Johnson

Printed in Hong Kong / China
1 2 3 4 5 6 7 8 9 05 04 03 02 01

Acknowledgments
We wish to thank the following individuals and organizations for their help and assistance and for supplying material in their collections:
AKG 2, 6, 9 bottom, 10, 13 bottom, 18 left, 23 top, 25 bottom; Art Archive 7 bottom, 13 top, 16 top; C M Dixon 3 top, 9 top, 12 top, 15 top right, 19 top, 30 top; Corbis 1 (Nik Wheeler), 3 (Enzo Ragazzini), 4 (Roman Souma), 5 (Roger Ressmeyer), 7 top (David Lees), 8 (Roger Wood), 10-11 (Nik Wheeler), 11 (Ruggero Vanni), 12 (bottom), 15 bottom (Sean Sexton Collections), 16 bottom (MIT Collection), 20 top (Gianni Dagli Orti), 21 (Enzo Ragazzini), 27 (Diego Lezama Orezzoli), 28-29 (Charles Lenars); Robert Harding 14, 17; Rex pictures 15 top left; South American Pictures 18 right, 19 bottom, 23 bottom, 24, 25 top; Tony Stone 20 bottom, 26; Topham 22; Werner Forman 30 bottom. All artwork by Michael Posen.

▶ (Top) This gold figure was found in Colombia, where the legend of El Dorado began. (See page 18.)

▶ (Bottom) The ruins of the South American city of Tikal can be seen through the thick jungles of Guatemala. (See page 20.)

◀ This golden bull, and its beard made of precious stones, decorate a musical instrument. The harp was found in the ancient city of Ur. (See page 6.)

CONTENTS

 LOOK FOR THE LOST-CITY BOX

Look for the black ruins sign in boxes like this.
Here you will find extra facts, stories, and other
interesting information about lost cities.

LOST CITIES

How can a city become "lost"? Can you imagine
Chicago or New York ever disappearing?
It seems impossible. But that is just what happened
to some cities in the past. Cities that were once
home to thousands of people were abandoned.

▼ This map shows
some of the lost cities
of the world.

▼ The ruins of the Inca city
of Machu Picchu lay hidden
in the mountains of Peru
for nearly 400 years.

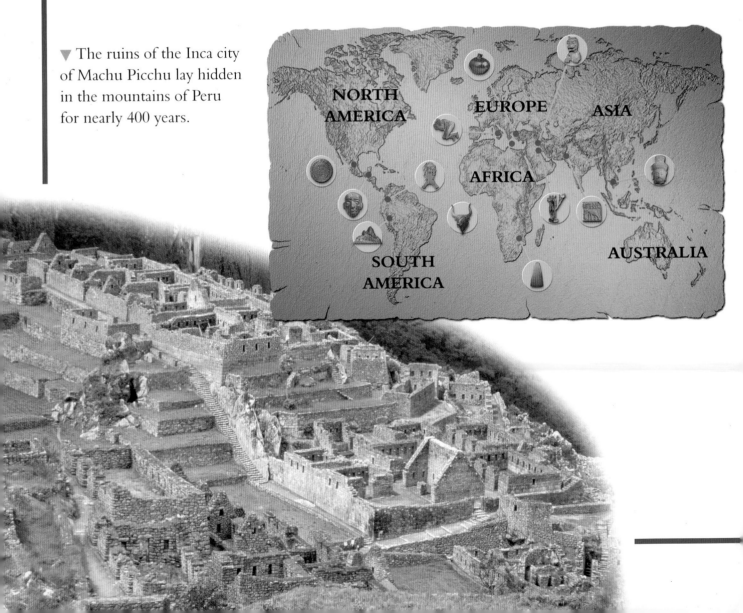

NORTH
AMERICA

EUROPE

ASIA

AFRICA

SOUTH
AMERICA

AUSTRALIA

Some cities were left empty after the people who lived in them were defeated by enemies. Others were destroyed by natural disasters. For example, the city of Pompeii was part of the Roman Empire. The city disappeared when it was buried beneath the ash from a volcano.

▲ The city of Pompeii was covered by layers of ash when Mount Vesuvius erupted in A.D. 79 nearly 2,000 years ago.

 BENEATH THE WAVES

Over 2,000 years ago, a Greek writer named Plato wrote about an island called Atlantis. On the island was a fantastic city with temples, canals, baths, and race-tracks. But the gods grew angry with the people of Atlantis, and made the island sink beneath the waves. Did Atlantis really exist? Nobody knows.

Lost cities leave behind clues that tell people they once existed. Their ruins and treasures stay hidden beneath the earth for hundreds or thousands of years. Their names and stories live on in ancient books. From these clues, we can solve the mystery of a lost city.

THE CITY OF UR

The head of a bull decorates a golden harp that was found in the ancient city of Ur.

For thousands of years, a tower as tall as a skyscraper stood forgotten in the deserts of Iraq, in Asia. Then an English visitor dug into the earth and found some clay cylinders covered in strange, shaped writing.

The writing said that the tower had been built by King Ur-Nammu. In the Bible, Abraham comes from Ur. Was the tower part of his city?

In 1923 the archaeologist Sir Leonard Woolley solved the mystery. He dug tons of earth from around the tower and revealed the magnificent city of Ur.

 ## ROYAL GRAVES

Woolley discovered a royal graveyard at Ur. The graves contained harps, headdresses, and hairbands made from gold. There were also the skeletons of servants. They had been put in tombs with their dead king or queen before drinking poison from golden cups.

The city of Ur was over 4,000 years old, one of the oldest cities ever built. It was part of a land named Mesopotamia and people called Sumerians had lived there. The Sumerians had palaces and schools, plows, and wheeled wagons. They used arithmetic, calendars, and the earliest form of writing.

▼ This beautifully decorated box shows us what the people who lived in Ur might have looked like.

▼ The remains of walls show where the city of Ur once stood.

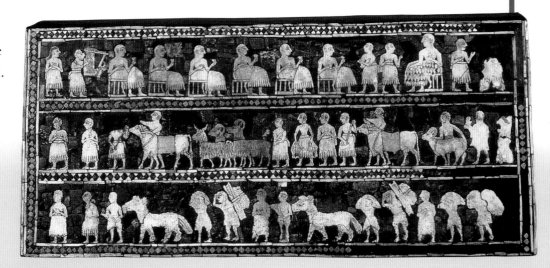

THE MONSTER OF KNOSSOS

Storytellers from ancient Greece have left us many wonderful myths. One famous story describes King Minos. He lived in a palace in the city of Knossos, on the island of Crete. In a stone maze he kept the Minotaur—a monster with the body of a man and the head of a bull.

Was this just a story? People thought so for many centuries. Then, in 1900 the English historian Sir Arthur Evans began digging into a grassy mound on Crete. He uncovered staircases, walls painted with beautiful pictures, and 1,400 different rooms. He had found the palace of King Minos.

▲ Tiles found at Knossos show us what the city's houses might have looked like.

THE CITY THAT SANK

Around 1450 B.C. a volcano erupted on the island of Thera (or Santorini), showering nearby Crete with ash. At this time, the Minoan kingdom came to a sudden end. Perhaps the Minoans were destroyed by this huge volcano. Some people even think the legend of Atlantis may be about the Minoans.

The palace's corridors twisted and turned, just like the maze in the story. There were also signs of the Minotaur. The walls were painted with men leaping over the back of a bull! So the myth described people who had really lived. Evans called them Minoans, after their king, Minos.

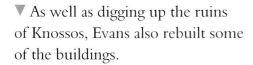 As well as digging up the ruins of Knossos, Evans also rebuilt some of the buildings.

▲ This picture of a boy leaping over a bull decorated one of the walls in the palace.

THE TOWER OF BABYLON

T he Bible tells how people in the ancient city of Babylon tried to build a tower high enough to reach heaven. God punished the people by making each builder speak differently. In this way the world's languages were created. Today we call this the Tower of Babel. But did the tower ever exist?

▲ This is an artist's idea of what the Tower of Babel may have looked like.

At the beginning of the last century, archaeologists dug beneath ruins near the Euphrates River in Iraq. They found old writing that told Babylon's history and the remains of the ancient city itself. They also uncovered the foundations, or base, of a pyramid that had once stood about 300 feet (91m) tall. They had found the Tower of Babel!

STOLEN BRICKS

More than 2,000 years ago, a Greek historian named Herodotus visited Babylon and said, "It surpasses [is greater] in splendor any city of the known world." He described the Tower of Babel, with eight stories and a temple at the top. But by 1900 all that remained was a ditch full of water. The tower's bricks had been stolen by local builders!

◀ All that remains of the Tower of Babel are its foundations.

▲ The beautiful Ishtar Gate has been rebuilt in a museum to look like it would have looked some 2,500 years ago.

Babylon was ruled by King Nebuchadrezzar in the sixth century B.C. The city was known for its riches. Visitors entered through the dazzling blue Ishtar Gate, decorated with carved bulls and dragons. The Hanging Gardens—one of the Seven Wonders of the Ancient World—were also in Babylon.

THE HORSE OF TROY

▼ This vase shows soldiers hiding in a wooden horse.

The city of Troy is the setting for the *Iliad*, a famous story by the ancient Greek poet Homer. It tells how a prince of Troy named Paris stole Helen, the beautiful wife of a Greek king.

The Greeks sent a thousand ships to rescue her. Then they surrounded and threatened Troy for ten years. Finally, the soldiers silently entered into the city hidden inside a wooden horse!

▼ Schliemann photographed Troy's treasures when he found them.

 MISSING TREASURE

Heinrich Schliemann dug up nearly 10,000 gold objects at Troy. He smuggled them out of Turkey to Germany. But at the end of World War II, they vanished. In the 1990s the treasure was found. It had been taken by Russian soldiers to Moscow, where it is now in a museum.

Could Troy have been a real city? A German archaeologist named Heinrich Schliemann thought so. He had read the *Iliad* many times and believed Troy once stood on a hill at Hissarlik, in Turkey. In the 1870s he dug a trench through the hill. By doing this, he uncovered the ruins of not one Troy, but many! The city had been destroyed and rebuilt again and again.

▲ Schliemann's greatest wish was to discover the lost city of Troy.

One layer of Troy's ruins contained storage jars for food and water, skeletons, and the marks of sling bullets and fire. These clues suggested there had been a siege and a battle—probably the one in Homer's story!

▲ Schliemann's workers found layer upon layer of ancient ruins.

POMPEII UNDER ASH

In 1594 builders were digging near Vesuvius, a volcano in Italy. They did not know that an ancient Roman city lay buried beneath their feet. Then they uncovered a stone with the Latin word for "Pompeii" written on it. What did this mean?

The mystery was solved in 1860 by Professor Giuseppe Fiorelli. He excavated the area and revealed the lost city of Pompeii. On August 24, A.D. 79, Vesuvius had erupted and buried Pompeii beneath tons of red-hot ash.

▲ After nearly 2,000 years, people can once again walk down the main street of Pompeii.

 ## BENEATH YOUR FEET

Many writers in ancient Rome recorded the tragedy of Pompeii. The words of a poet named Statius might describe all lost cities, "Will future centuries, when new seed [grass] will have covered over the waste, believe that entire cities and their inhabitants lie under their feet?"

▲ Corn was ground in these bakery mills, grinding stones, that were probably turned by donkeys.

▶ Fiorelli made this plaster model of a dog that was trapped by its chain as the ash covered it.

▲ This painting decorated the wall of a villa, or Roman house, in Pompeii.

The ash had kept the city just as it was before the volcano erupted. Fiorelli found graffiti on walls and food where it had been left on that day. This included eggs in a bowl, loaves in an oven, and olives on display in a shop.

Buried bodies had left hollow molds in the ash. Fiorelli filled these with plaster and created statues of the people of Pompeii in their last moments. A man had climbed into a tree, two children were hiding in a cellar, and a dog was trapped by its chain. The last moments of Pompeii were captured forever.

GREAT ZIMBABWE

In the Bible, King Solomon of Israel was said to have found great riches in a land called Ophir. When Portuguese explorers first sailed along the east coast of Africa in the 1490s, they found busy cities and ports where gold was traded. They also heard stories of Ophir, a land of gold.

◀ This painting shows King Solomon in his court.

▼ When explorers found the walls of Great Zimbabwe, they thought they had found Ophir.

Over 300 years later, a group of explorers headed inland. Suddenly their African porters sat down and began clapping. Before them, hidden by trees and vines, towered an enormous stone wall. A million huge stone blocks formed the circular wall. They had discovered the lost city of Great Zimbabwe.

▶ This mysterious stone tower stands inside the walls of Great Zimbabwe.

 CONE TOWER

Great Zimbabwe holds another mystery. Inside the main building, called the Great Enclosure, is a tower shaped like a tall cone and made of stone bricks. It has no way in or out and is totally solid. What could it have been used for? Nobody knows for sure.

Was Great Zimbabwe part of Ophir? Many people thought so. But Great Zimbabwe had actually been built for an African king, who traded gold for pottery and beads. The city could not be Solomon's famous land of gold because it had been built more than 2,000 years after Solomon's time!

THE LEGEND OF EL DORADO

In the 1500s Spanish armies in South America heard a strange story, or myth. It told of a king who covered his body with gold dust. He was said to have once sailed a raft across a lake, washed off the dust, then thrown emeralds into the water. His name was "El Dorado," or the Golden Man.

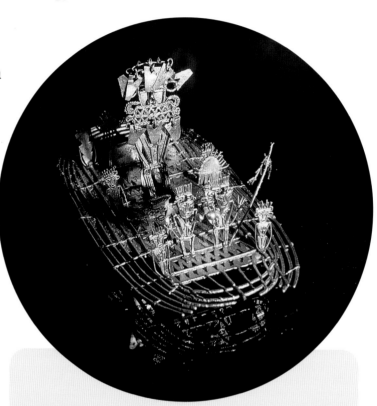

▲ Myths said that helpers covered El Dorado with glue, then blew gold dust all over him.

🏛 HEART OF GOLD

Christoper Columbus, who sailed to America in 1492, wrote, "Gold is the most exquisite [beautiful] of all things. Whoever possesses gold can acquire [get] all that he desires in the world. Truly, for gold he can gain entrance for his soul into Paradise." The explorers who hunted for the place called El Dorado thought so, too.

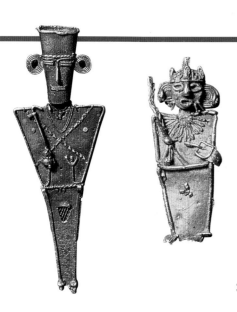

◄ These beautifully made "golden men" were found in tombs in Colombia.

But some said El Dorado was a city made of gold. Greedy Spanish soldiers rushed to find the golden city. They killed thousands of people in their search for the treasure.

The mystery of El Dorado was solved at Lake Guatavita, in Colombia. The Muisca people lived on its shores, and they were brilliant goldsmiths. When the Spanish made them drain the nearby lake with buckets, they found an emerald as big as an egg. Centuries later a golden sculpture of El Dorado on his raft was found in another lake. The truth was that El Dorado was just a king, not a city.

◄ This gold sculpture of El Dorado was found in a lake in Colombia.

▼ Here at the huge Lake Guatavita, gold-covered kings were said to have swum in the lake's water.

THE PYRAMIDS OF TIKAL

For 600 years, the Maya lived in cities in Central America. They were brilliant astronomers, who studied the stars and planets. Between 40,000 and as many as 100,000 people lived in Tikal. In the thick jungle of Guatemala, it was a grand city of palaces, temples, and pyramids. The pyramids were painted in bright colors.

▼ Jungle hides nearly all of the ruins of the city of Tikal.

▶ This sculpture shows a Mayan ball player.

PLAYING TO WIN

Among the ruins of Mayan cities are the huge, sloping walls of "ball courts." Here the Maya played a strange ball game called *pok-ta-pok*. This ballgame was a very serious game for the Maya. Sometimes the losers were sacrificed, or killed to please, the gods!

In A.D. 900, Tikal was suddenly abandoned. The jungle grew where the city had been, and animals walked through the once busy streets. But still the tops of the pyramids peered over the treetops.

In 1848 explorers cut away the jungle to find Tikal. Although the brightly painted walls had faded to gray stone, the huge pyramids and temples still towered over the jungle. Why did the Maya leave this magnificent city? That mystery has never been solved.

▲ The jungle has been cleared away. Now we can see the pyramids of Tikal.

THE SKULLS OF TENOCHTITLÁN

In 1519 the Spanish adventurer Hernán Cortés led his soldiers across Mexico to Lake Texcoco. There he saw a floating city of white stone. It was decorated with millions of flowers. Houses circled an area filled with palaces and pyramids.

The city had a zoo full of wild animals. People traveled around the city in boats, on canals instead of roads. Three main bridges led to the shore.

▲ This scary Aztec mask is made out of a human skull and decorated with blue stones.

THE AZTEC EAGLE

In their myths, a god told the Aztecs to build a city where they saw an eagle sitting on a cactus and eating a snake. They saw the eagle at Lake Texcoco and built Tenochtitlán. Today the eagle, snake, and cactus are on the national flag of Mexico.

Tenochtitlán was the capital city of the Aztecs. They were brave warriors who ruled a kingdom of millions. But the city held a mystery. The Spaniards saw temple walls covered with blood. They counted 136,000 human skulls, shown for all to see on a rack! The horrified Spaniards discovered that the Aztec priests killed people to please their gods.

◀ You can see Tenochtitlán's bridges to the mainland in this painting.

The Aztecs believed Cortés was himself a god and welcomed him. But within two years Cortés had destroyed Tenochtitlán and stolen its riches. Today its ruins lie buried beneath Mexico City.

▼ This is a copy of a skull rack from one of Tenochtitlán's temples.

MACHU PICCHU

High up in the Andes Mountains of Peru is a ruined city that looks like a fairy-tale castle. The clouds drift among the ruins of white granite temples, palaces, and fountains. The hillside is carved into steplike fields, like a giant's staircase. The people that once lived there grew their crops and kept their animals on these fields.

▼ The Inca city of Machu Picchu was so well hidden that Spanish invaders never found it.

◄ This temple at Machu Picchu was built with different-shaped stones.

MUMMY

A mysterious room under the Temple of the Sun at Machu Picchu has stairs leading nowhere. The room may have been where the Incas kept their dead emperors. The Incas made their dead rulers into mummies. They dressed them, seated them on thrones, and even took them on visits to other mummies!

This lost city of Machu Picchu was discovered in 1911 by the American explorer Hiram Bingham. It was once the secret city of the Inca people. In the 1400s they ruled the largest empire in America. They believed that their mighty emperor was a god. He was worshiped by the 12 million people in his empire.

▼ In Peru, people placed gold masks like this one on the faces of mummies.

Machu Picchu has many mysteries. The Incas had no wheels, but somehow they could move stones bigger than a man. They had no iron tools and no cement, but they made walls of stone that still stand today. Even earthquakes cannot destroy them!

FACTS ABOUT LOST CITIES

Here are some interesting facts and figures about lost cities.

The first city
The ruins of the oldest lost city were found at Catal Hüyük, in Turkey. They are about 8,000 years old. Its people collected glass from volcanoes to make tools!

The first writing
The oldest writing in the world was found on clay tablets at Uruk, a Sumerian city in Mesopotamia. It dates back to before 3000 B.C.

ANGKOR WAT

The biggest temple in the world is Angkor Wat. It is bigger than Vatican City in Rome. It is part of the lost city of Angkor, buried in the jungles of Cambodia.

Wheels in motion
Wheels were first used to make pottery and for transportation more than 5,000 years ago in Sumerian cities such as Ur and Uruk.

Fun and games
Beautiful carved wooden boards found at Ur and Knossos show that both the Sumerians and Minoans enjoyed board games.

▲ These men are sitting underneath beautiful carvings at the ruined city of Angkor.

An early bath
There was a giant tub at the center of Mohenjo-daro. This city in the country we call Pakistan dates back to 2500-1500 B.C.

Lap of luxury
The palace at Knossos had a clever system of pipes and sewers. These provided running water and a toilet that could be flushed.

Smell of success
Babylon's gardens were perfumed by at least 70 different herbs.

Wonderful wall
Babylon was protected by 7 miles (17 km) of walls. They were so thick that a chariot pulled by four horses could travel along the top.

Wooden horse

Here is the first picture showing the wooden horse the Greeks used to capture Troy. It is on a vase that was found on a Greek island.

Ancient tales

Heinrich Schliemann found the lost city of Troy. He was buried with copies of Homer's poems the *Iliad* and the *Odyssey* on his coffin.

Lost sheep

The volcano that covered Pompeii in ash was not the first disaster to hit the Italian city. In A.D. 62, an earthquake caused 600 sheep to disappear through a crack in the ground!

Inner city

The Maya did not believe in knocking down houses and palaces. They just built on top of them. Some buildings at Tikal have more than ten smaller ones inside them.

▲ The ruins at Mohenjo-daro in Pakistan are around 4,500 years old. Among them is a giant bathtub.

Hidden gods

In 1978 a stone three times the height of a man was dug up in Mexico City. It was beautifully carved and showed the body of an Aztec goddess whose arms and legs had been cut off.

Catching the sun

A special stone at Machu Picchu was called Intihuatana. That means "place to which the sun is tied." The Inca worshiped the sun, which at certain times of the year is so low that it appears to touch this stone.

 LOST-CITY DATES

City name	Who lived there?	When?	When was it found again?
Ur	Sumerians	3500–2000 B.C.	1923
Knossos	Minoans	2000–1400 B.C.	1900
Babylon	Babylonians	1800 B.C.–A.D. 100	1899
Troy	Trojans/Greeks	1700 B.C.–A.D. 500	1871
Pompeii	Romans	500 B.C.–A.D. 79	1860
Great Zimbabwe	Shona	A.D. 1100–1500	1868
Tikal	Mayas	A.D. 300–900	1848
Tenochtitlán	Aztecs	A.D. 1325–1521	1978
Machu Picchu	Incas	A.D. 1400–1532	1911

WORDS ON LOST CITIES

◀ Thousands of stone seals like the ones shown on this page were found among the ruins of Mohenjo-daro.

This glossary explains some words used in this book that you might not have seen before.

abandon (uh-BAN-duhn)
To leave something or someone behind.

archaeologist
(ar-kee-OL-uh-jist)
Someone who studies history by looking at the ancient remains of buildings, tools, jewelery or other things.

astronomers
(uh-STRON-uh-murs)
People who study the sun, moon, planets, and stars.

canals (kuh-NALZ)
Rivers or waterways that are not natural. These waterways are but built by people.

cylinder (SIL-uhn-dur)
A long object with straight sides and a rounded shape. A drainpipe is a cylinder.

empire (EM-pire)
A group of countries or people ruled by one person who is usually called an emperor.

enclosure (en-KLOH-zhur)
An area surrounded by a wall or fence.

excavate (EK-skuh-vate)
To dig up or uncover something from the earth. Lost cities, for example, are excavated by archaeologists.

exquisite (ek-SWIZ-it)
Something that is beautiful and delicate.

goldsmiths
(GOHLD-smiths)
Craftsmen who are skilled at making items from gold.

granite (GRAN-it)
A very hard, heavy type of rock, often used in the construction of buildings and monuments.

 SEVEN WONDERS

Seven of the world's greatest buildings in ancient times were called the Seven Wonders of the World. The list varies, but it sometimes includes the pyramids of Egypt; the Hanging Gardens of Babylon; the Temple of Artemis in Ephesus, Turkey; the Statue of Zeus at Olympia, in Greece; the Mausoleum, a tomb at Halicarnassus in Turkey; the Colossus, a statue on the Greek island of Rhodes; and the Lighthouse of Alexandria on the Egyptian island of Pharos.

Each of these tablets shows a beautifully carved animal next to an early form of writing.

inhabitants
(in-HAB-i-tinss)
The people who live in a place, for example in a city.

invaders (in-VADE-urz)
People or armies who enter the land of their enemies to attack them.

Mesopotamia
(mess-OH-poh-TAME-ee-uh)
An ancient country in southwest Asia, between two rivers, the Tigris and Euphrates. Some of the oldest cities were built in Mesopotamia.

mummies (MUH-meez)
Dead bodies preserved by drying, wrapping in bandages, or adding chemicals, so that the skin does not rot away as it does on a normal dead body.

myth (mith)
A legend or story, sometimes mixing a made-up story with real facts. Myths often have a religious meaning.

preserve (PREE-zurv)
To stop something from rotting by using chemicals or herbs to make it last or by drying it.

sacrifice (SAK-ruh-fise)
When something or someone is killed to please the gods.

siege (seej)
When a city that is built like a fort is surrounded and attacked by enemies.

surpasses (sur-PASS-ez)
When something is greater or better than something else.

tablets (TAB-lits)
Blocks of stone or wood that are used to write or draw on by carving into them.

PROJECTS ON LOST CITIES

If you want to find out more about lost cities, here are some ideas for projects.

BECOME AN ARCHAEOLOGIST

The lost cities in this book are on the other side of the world. But you might be surprised at how much history you can find in your own town or city. You may find ancient trails of the Native Americans or a Pueblo! Ask at your nearest library if there is a local studies center or group. They should also know if there is an archaeological society that will let you join in a dig. Then you can try out the techniques used to discover Troy.

▲ This gold helmet from Ur is in the British Museum.

▶ This crown was found in the royal tombs of Ur.

 ## SEE THE TREASURE

Some ancient treasures found are in large museums like the Smithsonian Museum in Washington, D.C., or the Metropolitan Museum in New York. These collections hold or show treasures from the Egyptian pyramids, from Africa and Asia, Greece, and Cyprus. Some are from the sites of cities lost long ago.

PLAN A CITY

There are many books and websites about ancient cities. Choose your favorite lost city and try to find as much information about it as you can. You might be able to find diagrams, maps, measurements, and photographs of your lost city. When you have gathered as many details as you can, try to draw a plan of the city. Use a large sheet of square paper and different colored pencils to show all the different features of the city.

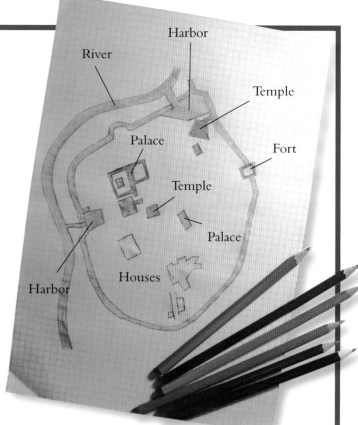

▶ A plan of the ancient city of Ur, in Mesopotamia

Lost Cities on the Web

If you have access to the Internet, you may be able to track down information including photos and plans of ancient cities and pictures of some of the treasures found there. Here are a few lost-city websites to try:

http://fluid7.demon.co.uk. Wander through the ruins of Machu Picchu.

http://www.sci.mus.mn.us Have an adventure with the Maya. The site includes some brilliant photos of the temples of Tikal, and you can keep a logbook of your travels.

http://www.culture.gr Visit the palace of Knossos and see the amazing wall paintings.

http://pages.ancientsites .com/~/nebuchadnessar/ jojo/RoyalTombs.html

Enjoy photographs of objects from the royal tombs of Ur. These are things that Leonard Wooley uncovered.

Remember that the Web can change, so don't worry if you can't find these websites. You can search for other lost-city sites using any search engine. Try using the search phrases "lost cities," "ancient cities," or just the name of a city you want to study.

INDEX